THE
POWER
OF
WISDOM

Prakash Press

THE

POWER

OF

WISDOM

When You Change
How You See the World,
Your Whole World Changes

Aman Motwane

Prakash Press

Prakash Press
P.O. Box 8004
Redondo Beach, CA 90277

Library of Congress Cataloging-in-Publication Data

Motwane, Aman,
The Power of Wisdom:
When You Change How You See The World,
Your Whole World Changes
p. cm.
ISBN 0-9671350-1-X hardcover
1. Success in business. 2. Interpersonal relations. 3. Self-management.
4. Peace of mind. 5. Conduct of life. I. Title.

"Never does nature say one thing
and wisdom another."
Juvenal

WHEN YOU CHANGE
HOW YOU SEE THE WORLD,
YOUR WHOLE WORLD CHANGES

Aman Motwane
The Power of Wisdom

"We do not see things as they are; We see things as we are."

Talmud

"The way we see things is the source of the way we think and the way we act."

Stephen Covey
The 7 Habits of
Highly-Effective People

"If you change your perception, you change the experience of your body and your world."

Deepak Chopra, M.D.
Ageless Body, Timeless Mind

"Those who see that no one else sees — these people will dominate the future."

FORTUNE magazine
The Most Valuable Quality

Table of Contents

Introduction

"Will I *ever* find lasting success and happiness?"

This question has reverberated through our minds for thousands of years. We have searched for the answer in our various roles — parent, lover, spouse, employer, employee, co-worker, leader, business executive ...

To find the answer, we have sought gurus, experts, therapists and consultants; learned skills, tricks and techniques; adopted habits, behaviors and positive attitudes; changed jobs, relationships and even cities; jumped from one fad to another; tried new technologies, new tools and new psychologies.

We have poured so much energy into changing our world, we have completely overlooked the answer, perhaps because it is blinding in its simplicity —

> In order to change our world, we
> must first change how *we see the*
> *world.*

How we see the world is the ultimate source of everything that happens to us. It shapes how we think ... which shapes how we act ... which ultimately shapes the quality of our results and our relationships.

Each of us already has the ability to see the world in such a way that it brings us the lasting results and relationships we desire. All we have to do is see the world *as it really is.* It is as simple as that.

Most of us are not aware that we don't see the world as it really is. We assume we do — but we actually see what is *easy* to see, or what we want to see, or what we think others want us to see. Inevitably, we build our life on a foundation of false assumptions. We attack symptoms rather than solve the underlying problems. And when our solutions don't stick, we are quick to blame the world around us.

Change how you see the world and your whole world will change. Look at things as they really are

— and you will see your problems, challenges and opportunities in a completely new light. You will discover within a fountain of clarity, creativity and insight that you never knew you had.

Although you may not realize it, you have already seen the world as it really is. As newborn children, we gazed upon the world with complete innocence and without the internal dialog that contaminates our perceptions today.

As we grow older, many of us come full circle and *once again* see the world as it really is. With age, we give up the struggle to control. We reconcile ourselves to seeing things the way they are. This is conventionally known as "gaining wisdom."

But you don't need age or experience to gain wisdom. You can see the world as it is, starting today.

Open your eyes. Observe nature. Everything, from a blade of grass to an erupting volcano, gives us a vital clue to the way things are. What nature teaches is basic and fundamental to life. It is the key to thriving and surviving with everything — relationships, parenting, leadership, team-building, stress-reduction, entrepreneurship, strategy-setting and waking up your inner creativity. Even the world's great religions, at their core, emulate nature's teachings — because nature's truths are impossible to deny.

Learning to see things as they are is a fascinating, glorious journey. There are seven steps to take — and with each step, a new light turns on inside. Everything feels the same and familiar, yet somehow wonderfully different and infinitely more powerful.

Come, let's embark on this wondrous journey …

The Wisdom

of

Duality

*Nothing exists
without its opposite*

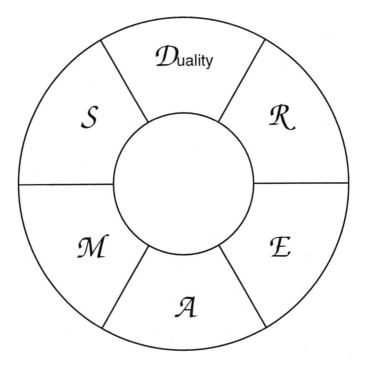

*Nature does have manure
and she does have roots
as well as blossoms*

*and you can't hate the manure
and blame the roots
for not being blossoms.*

R. Buckminster Fuller

The first step to waking up your inborn wisdom is recognizing the intrinsic Duality of the universe.

You may not realize it, but all the disappointments, frustrations, sufferings and anxieties in your life today have their origin in how you see the world.

You also may not realize that the fastest, easiest, most spontaneous and most natural way to achieve everything you desire is to change how you see the world.

All you have to do is give up your idealized vision of yourself and the world — and look directly at reality.

When we are blind to reality, we create our own misery and disappointment. Most of us are not even aware of our distorted perspective because it is part of our social conditioning. If we are aware of it, we believe it does not influence our life in any way. *But it does.*

To understand the hidden turbulence our perspective unleashes into our life, stand back for a moment and witness how you perceive a simple coin. Then, compare it to the reality of the universe.

As a result of our conditioning, most of us see everything as singular, unrelated, independent or separate. When we look at a coin, we tend to focus on the side that is up — heads or tails. We don't pay attention to the fact that both heads and tails are inseparable aspects of the same coin. We only see one side of the total picture. And this incomplete perspective severely limits what we think, decide, do or say.

The reality of the universe is that *nothing* exists without its opposite or complement. This is the Wisdom of Duality.

This simple change in perspective seems inconsequential, but it is tremendously empowering because it puts you in harmony with the way things really are. It is your foundation for waking up your inborn wisdom — and a necessary first step to fulfilling your dreams and realizing the abundance nature intended for you.

In nature, everything exists *because* of its opposite. The north pole exists *because* the south pole exists. Without hot, there would be no cold;

without black, no white; without weakness, no strength; without sadness, no joy; without failure, no success; without pain, no pleasure; without dark, no light.

Each unequivocally depends on its opposite for its existence and is manifest only *in contrast* to its opposite.

This simple insight empowers you in three ways:

First, you discover the key to realizing your highest potential.

Second, you see your optimal path for cementing your relationships.

And the third revelation of the Wisdom of Duality navigates you through the maze of conflicting advice and information that blurs the landscape of the Information Age.

Your Universe:
Expectations and Reality

The first revelation of the Wisdom of Duality is your key to realizing your highest potential.

In nature, we never expect to see a rose without thorns, nor spring without winter — not even a cow without dung.

Yet when it comes to ourselves, we secretly expect to be perfect, flawless, unblemished. We chastise every mistake unforgivingly. We become our biggest critic.

Without even realizing it, we expect to be what simply never exists in nature.

Nature's perfection comes from its *im*perfections. A blue sky becomes idyllic when blemished with clouds. A gentle breeze becomes melodious when mingled with the rustle of leaves. A calm ocean becomes mesmerizing when ravaged by crashing waves.

In the same way, your true beauty emerges from

the unexpected yet tender coexistence of strengths and non-strengths.

If you want to attain your highest potential, then make the commitment to view yourself through the prism of Duality. Drop your expectations. Stop the internal dialog that constantly evaluates and silently corrodes.

See yourself just as you are — a raw bundle of strengths and non-strengths. See yourself *completely*.

Your Universe:
Strengths and Non-Strengths

When you see yourself completely, without judgment or expectation, you will realize that many of your non-strengths are really strengths in disguise.

Strengths are situational. In other words, what appears to be a non-strength in one situation is actually a strength in another.

Cow manure is initially repulsive. Yet, when the situation is changed, it is an important source of fuel and fertilizer.

Your Universe:
Uniqueness and Greatness

In nature, no two snowflakes, no two fingerprints, no two sunsets are ever alike. It is pointless comparing one to another to decide which is better.

In the same way, your individual combination of strengths and non-strengths is totally unique.

You are inferior to no one. Don't waste time or energy trying to *measure up*.

You are also not superior to anyone. Don't waste time or energy trying to *affirm your superiority.*

You are just you. There is no other you. And your uniqueness — your "YOU-ness" — is the key to your greatness.

Get started now on a journey of knowing and understanding yourself. *Know yourself completely before you try to know anything else.*

Know what you are *wired* to do — what is so intrinsic to your nature that you could do it with your eyes closed. These are your strengths.

Know also what you are *not* wired to do — what is so alien to your nature that no matter how hard you studied it, you would almost never get it. These are your non-strengths.

Then hone your inborn strengths, sharpen them, make them constantly stronger. These abilities — these gifts — are your key to living an extraordinary life.

Look for situations that take maximum advantage of your innate abilities — both strengths and non-strengths. Avoid situations that call for abilities you clearly lack. Channel yourself where you know you will unequivocally shine — thus freeing the precious time and energy previously wasted pursuing illusions and false dreams.

The better the fit between your "YOU-ness" and your environment, the less you will need pep talks, motivational boosts, positive thinking, will power, self-improvement or attitude adjustment — all of which are little more than temporary, artificial props.

Your positive energy will come from within, from the excitement of knowing that success is inevitable — rather than from merely *thinking* positive.

YOUR UNIVERSE:
CONTROL AND SURRENDER

Often during the course of your life, you will find yourself in a situation that requires abilities you clearly lack.

When that happens, unabashedly and eagerly seek help from others. When you actively seek help to make your non-strengths irrelevant, nothing can hold you back. You are free to accomplish without limits or restraints. You are able to accomplish anything you want.

Most people secretly fear that such a matter-of-fact, realistic view of yourself — your highlights and flaws clearly on display — will push others away. But it actually draws them to you. In the eyes of others, only an individual who is truly real and authentic would have the courage to be so real and authentic. Only an individual who has a great internal reservoir of strength and a grounded sense of self would have the courage to be so open.

If you try to shield your non-strengths from others — if you try to control how others see you — you will unknowingly hinder your own success. Others will eventually see the real you. That's because your actions always speak louder than your words. Without realizing it, you will push them away. And without their help, you will be hard-pressed to make your non-strengths irrelevant.

Your Relationships:
Expectations and Reality

The second revelation of the Wisdom of Duality puts you on the optimal path for cementing your relationships.

Whether you admit it to yourself or not, your perspective of the people in your life — more than anything else — governs the course of your relationships with them.

Most of us don't engage our Wisdom of Duality. This is why, during each encounter — and long after each encounter is over — we judge, categorize, classify and label others. We impose our own standards of character, morality, righteousness, honesty, integrity. We expect compassion, trust, loyalty — precisely the way *we* define it.

If you want your relationships to be mutual, intimate and fulfilling then make the commitment to view every individual who enters your life through the prism of Duality. Relinquish the need to change others to conform to your expectations. See the reality of their strengths and non-strengths, rather than your idealized version of them.

Your Relationships:
Equality and Individuality

Every individual has hidden within him an infinite reservoir of pure potential — yet this potential remains frustratingly inaccessible for most, if not all, of his life.

The moment you start seeing another individual *completely*, you throw open the floodgates to realizing this life-enriching potential. You trigger an avalanche of pure joy and the deepest level of fulfillment into that individual's life.

This results in an unbreakable bond between you — and a chain reaction of mutual rewards.

How can such a simple change in perspective possibly lead to such a vibrant result?

The answer is displayed abundantly in nature.

In nature, every living entity thrives with vibrant life when its surrounding environment is perfectly suited to its *specific* individual characteristics.

An acorn will sprout into a majestic oak tree when the soil has just the right acidity, the air is just the right temperature, the water has just the right minerals.

A gardener who tailors his efforts *individually* to the *individual* needs of a rose bush in its *individual* environment will be rewarded with a burst of energetic growth.

The gardener who treats all the plants in his garden *equally* ultimately damages them — he either over-waters or under-waters, either over-fertilizes or under-fertilizes.

The rose bush gets infected, starts rotting — and struggles to survive.

The end result is often as though the gardener had done nothing at all. All of his efforts are completely wasted. All of the exquisite potential of the delicate rose bush remains completely repressed.

Conventional wisdom says treat everyone equally. But conventional wisdom insults nature's intelligence. If you want your relationships to be mutually satisfying and mutually rewarding, see every individual individually.

This simple perspective is the humble seed that blossoms every kind of relationship — between lovers, between spouses, between friends; and also, between parent and child, employer and employee, company and customer.

When you see another person completely for the individual he is, you effortlessly nourish him into realizing his unrealized potential.

YOUR RELATIONSHIPS:
COLLABORATION AND CO-EVOLUTION

Seeing others completely also leads to realizing *your own* unrealized potential — with almost dizzying speed.

This occurs through a simple but dynamic process that is a natural part of the universe.

In this process, every living entity that collaborates with other entities in the universe evolves faster and faster even as it expends less and less energy — while other entities that don't collaborate become increasingly inefficient and eventually perish.

Your existence on this planet is the result of such

a collaboration. It is the exquisite symphony between the plant kingdom and the human species, where humans inhale oxygen and exhale carbon dioxide, while the plant kingdom does the opposite — inhales carbon dioxide and exhales oxygen.

This connection between humans and the plant world is effortless and frictionless. It is the lifeblood and the necessary foundation for the co-evolution and survival of both humans and plant life.

You can tap the dynamic energy of collaboration and co-evolution in your own life by viewing yourself and everyone around you through the Wisdom of Duality.

When viewing yourself, just look for the answers to two simple questions:

Where do I need help from others?

What can I help others with?

When viewing another person, be aware of these same questions. Is this person requesting help in any way? If so, how can I help him?

The rest is as simple as the pieces of a jigsaw puzzle falling into place — you are one piece of the puzzle, someone else is the other piece. How can you best align *your* irregularities with *his* irregularities to form a complete picture? How can you collaborate and co-evolve — ultimately propelling *each* of you to realize your unrealized potential?

YOUR RELATIONSHIPS:
SIMILARITIES AND DIFFERENCES

The path of collaboration and co-evolution is the path through which everything in nature survives and thrives. That's because each entity participating in the collaboration doesn't have to be or do *everything*; he simply has to focus primarily on what he's already good at.

As the collaboration picks up steam, each person gets even better at what he's already good at. Ultimately, the partnership becomes so formidable that it can accomplish anything it sets its mind to.

Two people in such a collaboration can accomplish what ten, even a hundred, cannot independently.

But the key to such a formidable collaboration and co-evolution is not compatibility — it is the perfectly aligned *differences*.

If you want to create a fuller, richer life, relinquish your need to have friends and associates with whom you are always "comfortable." Stop seeking friends who are always "compatible" — who consistently share your interests, outlook and opinions.

Instead, look for your *opposite* in the people around you. Look for individuals that complement, rather than supplement, your skills and views. Deliberately go outside your circle of comfort. Cherish devil's advocates. Nourish mavericks. Embrace your differences.

YOUR RELATIONSHIPS:
THE CHICKEN AND THE EGG

Collaboration and co-evolution also give you an entirely new level of awareness of your role in your relationships.

In the symbiotic relationship between humans and plants, the relationship is so intricate and inextricable, it would be pointless to argue which is better — humans or plants, or which came first — oxygen or carbon dioxide.

In the same way, in your relationships, it is pointless to argue who is better or who is to blame or who started a conflict.

Instead, recognize that how the other person behaves with you is *inextricably* linked to how you behave with him. *How* you communicate with him sets the stage for *how* he responds to you.

You are not just the effect. You are *both* cause and effect. Whether you accept it or not, you *always* play a role in everything that happens in your life.

This is the reality of nature. A chicken is both the cause and the result of an egg. High tide not only follows, but yields to low tide.

Your Relationships:
Influencing and Leading

When you change how you view the people in your life, you automatically gain the power to influence them. This is the ultimate power because everything you want in life comes from them — your family, your friends, your co-workers, your boss, your associates, your customers.

With the Wisdom of Duality, this power is yours,

but not because you know all the right phrases and techniques, tactics and strategies.

Rather, you earn this power — and earned power is best because the people in your life feel completely *seen* by you. They feel safe with you. They feel nourished by you.

When a person feels completely seen, understood and accepted, he willingly opens up and becomes receptive to your caring influence and honesty. In return, he rewards you with the greatest gift from one human to another — energy and encouragement for fulfilling your own heart's desires.

Your Results:
Order and Chaos

The third revelation of the Wisdom of Duality navigates you through the maze of conflicting advice and information that blurs the landscape of the Information Age. You quickly identify the direct path to realizing your deepest desires.

Our world is so chaotic and unpredictable that we strive to gain a sense of order and stability. We sort things into clearly demarcated lines; write laws, policies, procedures; define acceptable and unacceptable behavior; form organization charts, groups, associations, families, nations. Then we develop maps, directories, programs and instructions to sift through and organize and package and label this chaos of information.

This helps us create order and to function socially. It is vital to our survival, and even to our success. But most people take these delineations too literally and rigidly, forgetting that these lines were *created in our minds,* with no basis in reality.

Nature does not share our need for boundaries. Nature does not care that we draw lines to separate California from Nevada ... or the U.S. from Canada. In nature, there is no fixed line of separation between the ocean and the sand, the hills and the valley, the tree and its roots.

In co-existence lies nature's most beautiful gifts. And her most breathtaking sights are visible, not at the peak of day or night, but at the magical confluence of the two — where day and night create dusk ... and night gives way to sunrise.

As nature embraces life without borders, so must you embrace life's predicaments, opportunities and obstacles with the same flexibility and fluidity.

YOUR RESULTS:
PROS AND CONS

Your enlightened view of the world is simply seeing life as it really is. And in so doing, you suddenly see opportunities that others can't.

Most people remain blind to the best opportunities because they've convinced themselves that two opposite ideas or concepts simply cannot coexist.

When life presents them with a choice between two alternatives, they forget that there's *always* a third, which is at the magical confluence of the two original alternatives.

They believe they must choose either short-term or long-term — but not both. They insist you must have autonomy or control — but not both. They think it's only possible to be independent or married — but not both.

What they don't realize is that by choosing one over the other, they deprive themselves of the key, life-nourishing benefits that are often available only through the unchosen path.

We all need to maintain our independence so that we don't lose ourselves in a marriage; yet, we *also* need the resurgent beauty of growing intimate with another soul.

We need to focus on the short term, because if we don't we will miss today; but we also need to take care of the long term, because if we don't we will miss tomorrow.

Don't limit yourself by choosing one over the other. Don't settle. Don't compromise. Stand back and look through the lens of Duality for a third, *higher* option, and this combined option will reveal itself to you *simply because you looked for it*, even if it was invisible and inaccessible at first.

Your Results:
Pleasure and Pain

Pleasure and pain are experiences of the heart. But they too, cannot exist without each other.

We struggle constantly to attain pleasure and *sustain* it. We struggle even harder to avoid *dis*pleasure. But our struggle is futile for it is against the truth of nature. Inevitably we are left frustrated, hopeless and empty.

What we don't realize is that our struggle does not come from life itself, but from our *flawed perspective* of life, and from our constant attempts to *force* life to match this flawed perspective.

Incorporate the Wisdom of Duality into your consciousness. Accept that pleasure and displeasure are inseparable. Recognize that in your pursuit of pleasure, you *will* encounter pain along the way. Embrace each situation *as it happens* and value each experience for its own sake rather than for the *feeling* it triggers.

Your Results:
Success and Failure

Without the Wisdom of Duality, we believe that people who are "successful" possess some mysterious inborn attributes and that people who are "failures" lack those same attributes.

With the Wisdom of Duality, you become aligned with the true origin of success and failure. You accept success and failure as merely different sides of the same coin and recognize that whenever you attempt something — at home, in love, at your job, in your business — the outcome is just as likely to be "win" as it is "lose." You never assign *meaning* to success or failure, to winning or losing.

Success is not triggered by some mysterious inborn attributes. It is triggered simply by the toss of a two-sided coin. And just as the outcome of each toss is random, so is your success or failure.

But behind that randomness hides a very interesting process ... and the *real secret to success*. Each time you toss that coin *again,* you give yourself yet one more chance to experience success.

If you want to geometrically multiply your chances of success, all you have to do is —

(1) toss your coin where you can play to your inborn strengths

(2) pay attention and look for what you can learn from each toss.

In the sixth wisdom, *the Wisdom of Stratification,* you will see the power of paying attention to the result of each toss. And in the seventh wisdom, *the Wisdom of Enlightenment,* you will see how simply introducing the desire to learn can spontaneously set you on your optimal path to success.

But first, you have to toss that coin again.

In essence, success is a game of numbers.

The fundamental difference between those who enjoy enduring success and those who struggle with failure is that successful people *play* this numbers game. And they play it *consistently.*

Like everyone else, they too experience failure and rejection. But they pay attention, learn and toss again — until the coin inevitably comes up a resounding "win."

Even after they attain worldly success, they don't stop tossing. Because they know the tide can and *will* turn the moment they stop, the moment they become complacent.

If you have been an abject "failure" until today, take solace in the Wisdom of Duality. Because starting today, you can transform yourself into a sudden success by simply deciding to toss that metaphorical coin one more time ... and then tossing it again, until you achieve the success you desire.

You really *can* go from failure to success overnight. Because this is what is intrinsic to nature.

Your Results:
the Right Way and the Wrong Way

From time immemorial, human beings have been searching for the one universal "best" way, the one universal "right" answer, for achieving their goals.

Our hunger for this universal solution has spawned an entire industry of experts, consultants and gurus who have made a career out of continually feeding us a new crop of relationship guides, diet programs, fitness revolutions, money-making secrets, management fads — each promised as *the* best solution. But these solutions are merely illusions because they ignore the reality of nature.

In nature, there is no right or wrong. Success paths are individual — just as individual as you and I.

There is no universal best way, no universal right answer. Despite what the experts proclaim, there are no specific characteristics that make a great leader. There are no specific personality traits that make a wonderful parent. There are no specific habits that make an effective person.

That is because what's best in one situation may or may not be best in another. What's best for one person may or may not be best for another person — and what's best for one person in a specific situation today may or may not be best for that same person in that same situation tomorrow.

Great leadership as well as great parenting come from seamlessly adjusting to each situation. Effective people have a nimbleness that matches the fluidity of nature.

You might say, "Adapting to each situation sounds daunting." But you will find it can actually be quite automatic, even effortless; and results come much, much faster.

A gardener who applies a cookie-cutter solution to every task works extraordinarily hard — using a shovel is clumsy when he really needs a trowel. His tools, instead of helping him, slow him down.

To find and stay on the shortest path to your goals, remember the Duality of nature. Allow yourself to flex with the situation before you.

YOUR RESULTS:
GOALS AND STRATEGIES

The moment you introduce nimbleness and flexibility into your perspective, you are poised to achieve goals you may not have even imagined. This too, is a reward of the Wisdom of Duality.

In nature, the most extraordinary events and entities aren't planned — they just happen, unexpected and undeliberated.

History shows our most important innovations and discoveries have rarely been the result of someone deliberately setting out to make that specific discovery. Rather, they have been the result of someone seeing a latent or tangential potential *while they were in pursuit of something else.*

This is why those who doggedly pursue specific goals and strategies, vigorously focusing on their "vision" to the exclusion of all else, inadvertently *block themselves from greatness.*

In their earnestness to increase the predictability of life, they unknowingly reduce the probability of attaining their heart's desires. In their eagerness to achieve a preconceived outcome, they remain blind to the most dazzling and exciting opportunities before them.

The unpredictable nature of the universe is usually the key to transcending the ordinary and attaining the extraordinary. To rise above the ordinary, simply look at your goals and strategies through the prism of Duality. Focus on both *making* things happen and *letting* things happen.

Pursue the yellow brick road ahead of you, but always with an eye open for those unexpected, serendipitous side roads that lead to a golden highway.

Your Results:
Speed and Velocity

Without the Wisdom of Duality, most people hustle, scramble, struggle to attain their goals — but despite all their hurrying, they don't gain much ground over their competitors. That's because they think speed comes from doing what everyone else is doing — only faster.

They read the same books as everyone else. They launch the same initiatives as everyone else. They jump on the same fads as everyone else. They buy the same technology as everybody else. Any edge they muster over others is temporary at best. The competition inevitably catches up. The experts start touting a new initiative or a new technology, and the race begins all over again.

Recognize that if you follow the herd, you will always scramble. When everyone is rushing in one direction, look for a pathway in the *opposite* direction. Instead of following the rules, *break the rules*. Don't just play in the field with everyone else. Create a new field and *own* that field. In this way, you will speed ahead of others — even as you work less.

The Wisdom of Duality gives you a powerful foundation for creating your future. Now, you must build a powerful structure on this foundation. You must wake up the other six wisdoms in your life.

Accessing
THE WISDOM OF DUALITY

(1)   I will know myself completely before I try to know anything else.

(2)   I will gratefully accept everyone and welcome their uniqueness.

(3)   I will look for the role I play in everything that happens. I will view myself as not just the effect — but *both* cause and effect.

(4)   I will always focus on getting the total picture so I can see both sides of everything clearly.

(5)   I will make things happen. And at the same time, I will *let* things happen.

(6)   I will focus on my uniqueness — and carve out my own unique path to my own unique accomplishments.

The Wisdom

of

Resonance

*Step into
the rhythm
of life*

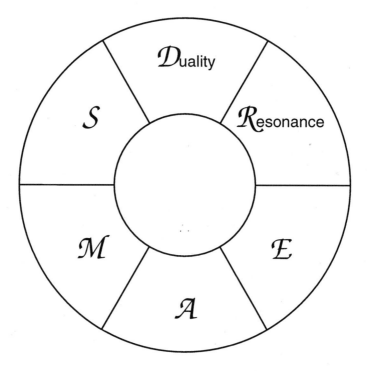

It is always sunrise somewhere ...
a shower is forever falling ...
vapor is ever rising ...

each in its turn,
as the round earth rolls.

John Muir

The second step to waking up your inborn wisdom is seeing the rhythm inherent in the universe.

This light reveals a new perspective and dimension and fortifies your ability to collect the accomplishments you desire.

Resonance is everywhere. It is the essence of life. It is how nature *gets things done* — smoothly and assuredly. When we learn this secret, we easily get what we want in life.

In nature, everything is dynamic — resonating, pulsating, oscillating, wiggling, flirting. Every cell is continually growing, mutating, morphing. Every atom, every molecule, every planet is circling incessantly around its nucleus.

The earth hurtles through space at the phenomenal rate of 64,300 miles per hour, and rotates on its axis at over 1,000 miles per hour. We don't *see* this incredible speed because from our vantage point, the ground is firm and steady — yet, the earth keeps rotating, revolving, resonating because this is nature's secret of *being*.

Resonance is nature's hidden but necessary lifeblood.

Because we usually cannot see the Resonance in nature, we are rarely aware of its genius — but if you observe *consciously*, you will see that *nothing* ever stops resonating.

What would happen if nature stopped resonating? Everything — including you and I and all our loved ones — would cease to exist.

This is why you must incorporate the Wisdom of Resonance into your perspective. It is essential for getting whatever you want in life.

Your Universe:
From Balance to Resonance

The first revelation of the Wisdom of Resonance shines a new light on your universe.

Our world pulls us in so many different directions that we strive to gain a sense of balance in our lives. We are constantly torn between our career and family; our aging parents and blossoming children; our wants and needs; our diets and cravings.

But our search for balance remains elusive — because in nature, there is no balance, no state of equilibrium, no perfect state of stability.

In nature, equilibrium and stability don't come from *being* at a perfect, balanced state — they come from resonating beautifully, harmoniously, peacefully *to* and *from* the ideal state.

This is demonstrated with a simple pendulum. A pendulum swings back and forth, back and forth — without ever standing still.

It flirts continually with the ideal, perfect position

where it would be completely vertical and "in balance" — but it never actually rests at that position.

This is the natural order of things. This is the way things *are*. This is reality. Everything else is simply our own *projection* of reality.

Most people choose to be guided by their own projection of reality. They choose to focus on the fact that they are *not* at the ideal, "perfect" state, never realizing that 99.9999999999999999+ percent of the time, it's impossible to be at that state. They doom themselves to a life of despair and inadequacy.

With the Wisdom of Resonance in your perspective, you see things the way they really are. Your compulsion to set things "right" evaporates. Your struggle to control vanishes. And this in itself, reduces the commotion in your life geometrically. Because once *you* stop interfering with the harmonic swing of your life, once *you* just let things be as they have to be, you remove the biggest source of agitation in your life.

Ultimately you reach a state where your life just swings synchronously, effortlessly, frictionlessly. And you become able to devote your time, money and energy to enjoying life — and its rewards — in totality.

YOUR UNIVERSE:
FROM UNCERTAINTY TO CERTAINTY

The constant swinging, twirling and circling of life appears to be the source of uncertainty — but really is the root of all certainty.

Resonance is how nature choreographs everything. Resonance is how nature *gets things done.*

Our heart within us beats, pulses and throbs incessantly — *and because it does*, our body is able to move, walk, run, jump ... and our mind is able to think, reflect, imagine, innovate.

The earth beneath our feet revolves and rotates incessantly — *and because it does*, seasons change and animal and plant life thrives.

Even nature's quartz crystal within a wrist watch pulsates and vibrates incessantly — *and because it does*, the watch shows time consistently and accurately.

Everything in nature has a scintillating rhythm — and this rhythm is the cause of everything. It sets the tone and pace for everything that happens.

It is the source of nature's momentum.

Nature gets everything done with remarkable speed — and this speed is effortless because it comes from the natural rhythm imbedded in everything.

Adopt this secret of nature and you too will guarantee results in your life with speed and certainty.

Synchronize everything you do with what you want. Set everything to move at a fast and steady rhythm — and this pace in itself will propel you forward, emulating the very way nature propels itself forward.

YOUR RESULTS:
FROM DESTRUCTION TO CONSTRUCTION

The second revelation of the Wisdom of Resonance is the key to raising yourself to a new plateau of accomplishment.

There is a very interesting process in nature for rising to such higher levels — unchangeably and unequivocally.

This stems from the same process nature uses to achieve a fast and consistent momentum — and keep life humming.

As you have already seen with *the Wisdom of Duality*, nature functions through the co-existence of opposites. Whenever you attempt to introduce a new order of things — the old way and the new way, old habits and new habits, old systems and new systems often tend to co-exist.

The lens of Resonance reveals that not only do the old and new co-exist, they inevitably yo-yo back and forth.

In other words, the forces of nature usually work *against* the new gaining a foothold. But occasionally, the cumulative energy of nature builds up so that the old gets wiped out and yields to the new. For example, hurricanes, floods, earthquakes and volcanic eruptions create the opportunity to start with "a clean slate." This is nature's secret for *making things happen.*

In nature, every new beginning is preceded by an ending. Every act of construction is preceded by an act of destruction.

A volcanic eruption devastates all plant life in its path — then the resulting ash becomes the fertile ground where new plants, previously crowded out, flourish.

A dazzling, fluttering butterfly emerges only when it leaves its life as a caterpillar behind.

If it is your desire to move from an old order of things to a new order of things, emulate nature's secret for making things happen. Deliberately destroy the old in order to be able to construct the new.

If you want to lose weight — and do it

permanently — it is not enough to eat slightly less every day. You will inevitably swing back and forth between dieting and splurging, between exercise and inertia.

To make your plan *stick*, first kill and bury your past image of yourself. Wipe the old you from your mind — only then will the new you be able to emerge.

Use this secret of nature to *reinvent* yourself and accomplishment will come spontaneously and inevitably.

With the Wisdom of Resonance in your perspective, you gain focus, pace and assurance for creating your future — and as long as you include the other wisdoms, nothing can stop you from fulfilling your desires.

Accessing
THE WISDOM OF RESONANCE

(1)   Today, I will review all my expectations. I will accept the reality that I will rarely achieve the so-called ideal of each of these expectations.

(2)   I will make sure my actions are synchronized with my intentions — and they are synchronized at a fast and consistent pace.

(3)   I will review those goals where I must close an old chapter to make it possible for a new one to start. I will accept that this is the only way I can rise to the higher plateau. I will make it clear to myself and others that going back to the old chapter is not an option.

The Wisdom

of

Ecology

*Every solution
contains the seeds
to a new problem*

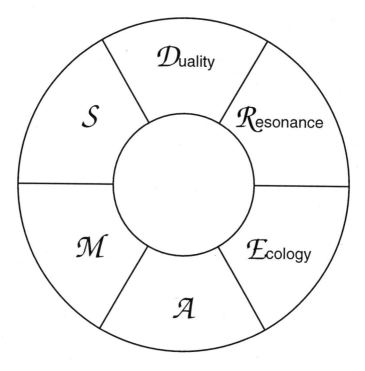

*The chief cause
of problems
is solutions.*

Eric Sevareid

The third step to waking up your wisdom is seeing that everything goes through a never-ending cycle.

Ecology is the relationship between humans and their physical and social environment. When you incorporate the Wisdom of Ecology into your vision, you see the true connection between you and your aspirations — and simply seeing this connection in itself dissolves the most formidable barriers to your goals.

In the scheme of nature, everything follows a vibrant, life-infusing cycle.

A drop of water on the ocean's surface evaporates to form a cloud ... falls back to earth as rain ... then returns to the ocean in a flowing river.

A tiny seedling germinates ... sprouts ... blossoms and sheds its seeds onto the soil ... and eventually returns to enrich the earth that gave it life.

The cycles of nature are manifest all around us — in a glistening drop of dew, the delicate petal of a rose, a tiny grain of sand, the iridescent hues of a rainbow, you, me.

Everything — every living organism, cell, atom, electron, planet, rock, even every thunderstorm and every weed — exists as part of a palpable, continuous cycle.

These cycles exist in perpetuity. They are necessary for survival. No one and nothing escapes it. Yet, we easily lose sight of its ubiquitous energy.

Everything that happens in your life, and the life of every human on this planet, is the result of one or more such cycles. You may not be conscious of them — but that does not mean they don't exist. In fact, they play a critical role in designing your future.

When you deny the existence of such cycles in your life, you struggle against the fundamental intention of nature. You unleash an infinity of turbulence, never realizing that your frustrations and disappointments are of your own creation.

When you see this cycle in its true pure form and embrace its existence, it becomes your ally — and your wisdom shepherds you to the fulfillment of your dreams and desires.

THE ADVANTAGE OF FORESIGHT:
BETWEEN STABILITY AND INSTABILITY

The Wisdom of Ecology gives you uncommon insight into your future — and there is no better advantage than foresight.

Our world is changing and evolving so rapidly that we steadfastly cling to anything that is even remotely predictable or stable. We are consumed by our search for security. Everything we do — the education we get, the careers we choose, the relationships we create — stems from a deep craving for reliability and certainty.

What we don't realize is that the kind of certainty we seek is nowhere to be found.

In nature, nothing seems certain. Nothing remains unchanged. Everything is constantly evolving — yet, hidden beneath all this apparent turmoil, is nature's own scheme for certainty.

Imagine a world in which the ocean→clouds→rain →river→ocean cycle suddenly stopped. The earth would become dry and parched. Plants would shrivel and die. Animals would dehydrate. Humans would wither away.

Nature's stability is created by *in*stability. Security is a direct result of *in*security. Certainty comes from *un*certainty.

We understandably want to believe that stability is the pillar of life — but the reality is that the *cycle of nature* is life.

Don't resist the waves of change. Stop looking at the world with worry, fear, anxiety. Instead, gaze upon your environment with unruffled equanimity — because the change and turmoil before you is your surest guarantee for the future.

Think of the future as a relentless river. Our immediate instinct is to protect ourself — to build a solid wall in its rapidly advancing path. But our wall, no matter how strong, quickly crumbles and washes away. There's only one sure way to protect yourself — build a raft that helps you float, flex and ride the turbulence.

When you get in step with the cycle of nature, the quality of your life — instead of being soaked with anxiety — will be showered with enthusiasm for the promise of the future.

THE ADVANTAGE OF FORESIGHT:
BETWEEN SOLUTIONS AND PROBLEMS

With the Wisdom of Ecology, you see nature's intelligence in the dance of the universe.

Most of us are on a constant quest to ease the tensions in our lives. We deploy innovation, machines and technology to solve our problems. We clamor for the day when things will get "better"— a better body, better job, better income, better relationship, better life. We are burdened with guilt and anxiety about missing out, becoming obsolete, simply being left behind. We are lured into a trivial dance to acquire the latest information, newest techniques, hottest gadgets — but nature is always one step ahead, racing to replace our old problems with new ones.

Imagine that every time you solve a problem, you scatter a thousand seeds into the sky. Some time in the future, in one nanosecond or perhaps several years, at least one of those seeds will germinate and sprout into a new problem — and this new problem will most likely be an *insidious version of your original problem.*

For example, e-mail was supposed to make us more efficient. But because sending e-mail is so easy, its sheer volume has inundated us and returned us to inefficiency.

There's nothing you can do to stop this problem→ solution→problem cycle. Like the weed→seed→ weed cycle, it is part of nature's scheme for the universe.

Weeds always return to a garden no matter how well you eradicate them. The job of weeding is never done. In the same way, problems always return, no matter how diligently you exterminate them.

Become conscious of this cycle, and you will harness its tremendous force and energy to gain a substantial personal advantage.

THE ADVANTAGE OF FORESIGHT:
BETWEEN SUCCESS AND FAILURE

When you have foreknowledge, rather than being just a pawn in the game of life, you become the master. Rather than falling behind the curve, you get ahead.

Every time you introduce a solution to a problem, all you have to do is *look* for a new problem to crop up.

Look for today's breakthrough to become tomorrow's entitlement. *Look* for today's discovery to become tomorrow's price of entry. *Look* for today's standard to become tomorrow's old news.

Look for your success today to become the *cause* of your failure tomorrow.

Conventional wisdom says, "Don't fix it if it ain't broke." With the Wisdom of Ecology, *look* for it to break on its own.

When you willingly enter this field of awareness, your path to an abundant future becomes crystal clear — because problems are really opportunities in disguise. Opportunities for getting ahead and *staying* ahead.

Put the cycle of your life in step with the cycle of

nature. Don't wait for others to raise the standards. Instead, *set* the higher standards. And even as you are setting this higher standard, prepare to introduce the *next* higher standard.

In this way, your experience of life will be filled with freshness and excitement, and the Wisdom of Ecology will become your wellspring of good fortune.

THE ADVANTAGE OF FORESIGHT:
BETWEEN TODAY AND TOMORROW

Nature doesn't just move in cycles — it moves through cycles in unpredictable ways.

Some years, the fury of winter arrives early, other years not at all; a series of merciless rain storms one year is followed by a defiant drought; spring's lavish display changes from year to year — lush yellow mustard this year, shimmering blue lupine the next.

Just as nature follows its cycle in unpredictable ways, so do humans and their relationships.

In our relationships, we look for stability and refuge from the rest of the world — but each human and each relationship operates on an individual cycle that surprises at every turn.

This is true for every type of relationship — parent-child, employer-employee, husband-wife, business-customer.

To enjoy a relationship that steadily becomes deep, meaningful and stable, *look* for others to raise their expectations continually, shift their priorities endlessly, change their preferences routinely.

When you give kindly and generously, be aware that it's a matter of time before your kindness becomes the new yardstick — and others simply expect *more* from you.

Don't become disgruntled or disillusioned by this seeming lack of gratitude. The wise gardener doesn't stop weeding just because he knows the job of weeding never ends.

When you incorporate this awareness into your perspective, your relationships, your results and your life will be elevated to a higher plane. You will still see the cycles inherent in life and the universe, but you will be increasingly shielded from its foam and froth. Your future will become increasingly certain — even as the tide of uncertainty continues lapping around you.

Accessing
THE WISDOM OF ECOLOGY

(1)   I will embrace change as part of the natural cycle of life. And I will look for ways to harness the power and energy inherent in this cycle.

(2)   I will actively anticipate the next step — and the step after that — even as I'm taking my current step. By my actions and decisions, I will lead the pack — instead of remaining a follower who always plays catch-up.

(3)   In all my relationships, I will anticipate change as a normal part of the cycle. I will look for priorities, preferences and expectations to continually shift.

The Wisdom

of

Aggregation

*We are all
ultimately connected*

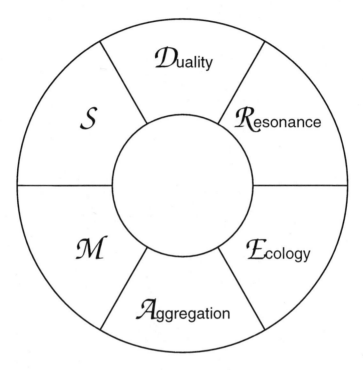

We are nature.
We are nature seeing nature.
The red-winged blackbird flies in us.

Susan Griffin

The fourth step to waking up your wisdom is recognizing that everything is ultimately connected.

Aggregate means a mass of distinct things gathered into a whole. With the Wisdom of Aggregation, you see the world around you as one interconnected, interrelated whole.

In our daily routines, it's easy to see everything as independent — a tree is unrelated to the birds in the sky or to the insects in the soil. You are unconnected to me.

But a tree depends on birds to propagate its seeds and on insects to aerate its soil. As for you and me, we are as different as two snowflakes — yet, at our core, we are the same. Our fears, confusions, desires and aspirations emanate from the same source within us.

At the core, everything is connected to everything else — and when you see these interconnections and interdependencies, you see what otherwise seems invisible, comprehend what otherwise appears incomprehensible, discern what otherwise remains indiscernible.

You gain both insight and foresight — insight into how to best dissolve your obstacles and foresight into the most lucrative opportunities ahead.

THE ADVANTAGE OF FORESIGHT:
SOAR LIKE AN EAGLE

The first revelation of the Wisdom of Aggregation gives you the advantage of foresight — you quickly see the hidden opportunities and obstacles ahead.

Everything in the universe, in its essential nature, is part of a bigger scheme. And the key to seeing what is really happening in any situation is to view everything in its larger context.

For example, a tree may appear isolated, but it affects and is affected by everything in its environment — sunshine, rain, wind, birds, minerals, other plants and trees, to name just a few. Look at the relationship between the tree and its environment and you will see the future of the tree.

Most people don't look for the big picture. They see only what is immediately visible. Without realizing it, they limit their own perspective. This is why they don't see the shortcuts around their obstacles, even though they are always available. They also miss tremendously rich opportunities, even though these opportunities are always within their reach.

Deliberately look for the big picture — just like an eagle that soars high above everything and scans the entire landscape. Maintain this overall perspective and you will uncover pathways and routes that most don't know exist. You will see roads to opportunities you never imagined possible.

THE ADVANTAGE OF FORESIGHT:
PEER BEYOND THE FAMILIAR

Another way people limit their perspective is by looking only at things that are familiar — and shielding out everything else. For example, a doctor may only read medical magazines, a movie buff may only search film websites, but not architecture sites.

Everything in nature is interrelated, which means that what is unfamiliar holds important clues about what is familiar. If you don't expose yourself to *both*, you will hinder your ability to see clearly.

You might believe you see everything, but still be

blind to the true relevance of what you see. You will easily miss the small, subtle nuances that can make a big difference. You will unknowingly overlook important options.

Break away from the artificial boundaries of the familiar and widen your circle. Embrace the unfamiliar — including people from different clubs, companies, industries, technologies, countries, philosophies, religions, functions, hierarchies.

The greatest opportunities and breakthroughs lie at the intersection of two *seemingly* unrelated areas. These opportunities are available for all to see. Yet most people don't see them simply because they think of everything as unrelated. But everything *is* related. To see opportunities that most never see, extend your perspective beyond the familiar.

The Advantage of Foresight:
Look for the Patterns

There is nothing complicated about the connections and interdependencies in nature.

Everything in the universe, from the tiniest cell to the largest planet, appears chaotic, random, intricate. But underlying this complexity lies an elegant simplicity. There's harmony behind the chaos, predictability behind the uncertainty, symphony behind the chatter.

For example, during the course of a day, you may witness a series of seemingly unrelated events — an apple falling from a tree, a river flowing towards the ocean, the changing of the tide. But look closely and you'll see that all of these events are orchestrated by the same unseen force — gravity.

Similarly, the night sky appears deep, fathomless, endless. Stars seem scattered haphazardly, each in its own private orbit, separated from other stars by hundreds, perhaps thousands, of light years. Yet, certain stars are always in the same formation. Throughout time, these patterns have helped navigate astronomers, astrologers, sailors, hikers and awe-struck night gazers.

Nature has a method to its madness. There's a pattern behind everything — and all you have to do is *look* for these patterns.

Imagine you are solving a jigsaw puzzle. If you look at each piece individually, all you will see is a random collection of pieces. And this fragmented perspective will slow you down.

But look at all the pieces *collectively*. Start with the assumption that all the pieces are interrelated and specifically look for how they fit together, and everything quickly falls into place.

You may not be aware of it, but every day you spontaneously recognize patterns. Most of us routinely read the facial expressions and behavior patterns of close family members. All of us respond instinctively to the colors on street lights — stop on red, go on green. And many follow the price patterns in the grocery store.

All you have to do is to raise these recognitions from the unconscious to the conscious. Instead of seeing patterns occasionally, deliberately look for them — and you will gain an understanding and appreciation of the universe as it really is.

THE ADVANTAGE OF FORESIGHT:
LOOK AT HUMAN PATTERNS

In the great interconnected soup of the universe, one key element weaves through practically every pattern of nature — human behavior.

Human behavior governs the pace and quality of nearly every event. For example, technology may move forward at breakneck speed, but ultimately the pace at which it becomes useful in the real world is limited by human acceptance.

This overarching pattern of human behavior affects everything — and fortunately, it is very *predictable.* That is because, through the ages, human behavior has not changed very much.

Humans have always had — and always will have — a deep-seated need to create order out of chaos, to create rules, maps, and hierarchies. We derive self-esteem from our status in society. We are territorial — we want "my territory" to be better than "your territory." We respond to perceived danger with "fight or flight." We crave to believe in something more powerful than ourselves. We desperately want to fit in. We often say one thing and do another.

To see these patterns, simply pay attention to what people do, rather than what they say. Rely less on data and more on behavior. Pay attention to *actions,* rather than opinions, memories or promises.

Once you include the patterns of human behavior

in your perspective, you will make a quantum leap in seeing what's really going on. And this will help you create any future you desire.

THE MAGIC OF INSIGHT:
LOOK AT THE CONNECTIONS

The second revelation of the Wisdom of Aggregation gives a deep and powerful insight into the true nature of people and events in your life.

Visualize a wave in the middle of the ocean. There is no way to isolate this wave from the other waves. It exists *because* other waves exist. Everything about this wave — the height of its ridge, the frequency of its swells, the shape of its curves — depends entirely on the characteristics of all the waves before it.

In other words, this wave is intricately and undeniably connected to an entire system of waves — and its behavior is influenced by this system. To understand how and why this wave behaves, focus on its underlying system.

In nature, no individual, no incident, no thought, no opportunity, no obstacle exists as an isolated element — each exists as part of its underlying system.

An extraordinary thing happens when you see the underlying system behind everyone and everything — most of the obstacles that have stubbornly hindered your progress simply disappear. That's because the vast majority of these obstacles are artificial — they exist because of our limited perspective.

With a limited perspective, we do not see the underlying cause-effect relationships. We are blind to the true source of our obstacle and squander our energies on the symptoms. We resort to judging, blaming, preaching, threatening — when often a simple change in the environment or system would quickly eliminate the problem. Without realizing it, we cause our problems to fester and grow.

Open your perspective. Look at everyone and everything as part of an aggregate whole. Seek the *fundamental* cause hidden in the aggregate, and you will gain an understanding so deep and complete, you will barrel past obstacles that used to stump you before.

The Magic of Insight:
Look at the Relationships

It has been said that every individual is the sum of his experiences, and indeed, every human being is the exquisite culmination of an infinity of decisions, choices, experiences and relationships that go back far in time.

If you want to be effective with every individual you encounter — whether friend, family, co-worker or customer — consciously look for the experiences and relationships that have shaped them.

As you have seen with the *Wisdom of Duality* and will see again with the *Wisdom of Magnanimity*, when a person feels seen and understood, they instinctively open up, and this mutual vulnerability is the necessary foundation for a long-lasting, meaningful relationship.

The Magic of Insight:
Look at Your Relationships

Like everyone else, you are the glorious aggregate of every experience and relationship.

Who you are at this present moment is exactly the

way you should be. Every breath, every decision, every moment from your past has been delicately orchestrated to bring you to this point.

If even one millisecond of your past had been somehow changed or different, everything about you in the present moment would be entirely different. That is because you would have had different experiences, made different mistakes, learned different lessons — and you simply wouldn't be the YOU you are today.

Rejoice the present moment. Rejoice every moment of the past that brought you to this moment. Regret nothing. Cherish everything.

Everything that happened in the past is part of your individual, personal and very special journey. These building blocks have intricately shaped your "YOU-ness." They are the reason you are now in the process of waking up your inborn wisdom.

From this moment forward, the experience of opening up your perspective will also shape you. It will shape how you think and how you act. Ultimately, it will shape your results and relationships. Rejoice — because no matter what else happens, no one can take that away.

Accessing
THE WISDOM OF AGGREGATION

(1)   I will reflect on the way I see the world around me. I will see beyond what's immediately visible and look for the underlying patterns.

(2)   In every decision I make, I will consider the basic patterns of human behavior, and how they affect my outcome.

(3)   I will look for the underlying cause-effect relationship behind all of my challenges and obstacles. I will look to fix the system, rather than blaming the people in the system.

(4)   I will reflect on how I view others. I will seek to understand them completely. I will pay attention to the experiences and relationships that shape their behavior.

The Wisdom

of

Magnanimity

*See through
your heart —
not your eyes*

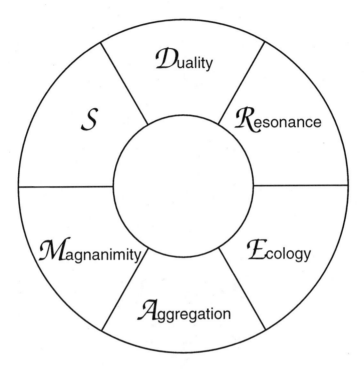

The world is so rich,
simply throbbing
with beautiful souls.
Forget yourself.

Henry Miller

The fifth step to waking up your wisdom is looking at each individual not with your eyes, but through your heart.

The word *Magnanimous* comes from the Latin *magnus* which means great, and *animus* which means soul. The Wisdom of Magnanimity reveals that the key to seeing the reality of others is to look at them through your heart and soul.

When you look at others with your eyes, you get a distorted perspective of their reality. You see only what appears on the surface — which rarely represents who they really are. But look at them through your soul, and you will *connect* with their reality. And this connection is key to everything you want in life.

Every life in the universe, no matter how strong and sturdy it appears on the surface, is delicate, fragile, uncertain.

Every acorn competes with other acorns, braces fires, droughts, insects, infections and wind. Simply taking root is a great triumph.

Every fish battles overcrowding, pollution,

dwindling food supplies and predators. Just surviving is a struggle.

Every person encounters fear, disappointment, frustration, competition and insecurity. Simply being seen and recognized is a cherished gift.

Incorporate the Wisdom of Magnanimity into your perspective and give this gift to everyone you encounter. See the inherent good in them. Recognize their innate desire to do their best. See their aspirations and their struggle to fulfill them.

This simple change in how you see others changes you. It changes how you think of them, what you say to them, and how you speak to them. You stop doing things *to* them — and instead, start doing things *with* them and *for* them.

You grow to genuinely care about them, which leads them to care about you in return. You willingly help them with their aspirations, which leads them to help you with yours. In this way, you build a powerful foundation of mutual affinity, commitment and success.

Your Relationships:
Strength Breeds Strength

Some might think that seeing others through the heart is soft and mushy — but it is actually the opposite. Seeing others through the heart requires a solid foundation of inner strength. You must first acknowledge your limitations, and recognize that you need the mental and emotional commitment of others to accomplish your goals. Once you are grounded in your own humanness, you will be able to see others through your heart, and empathize with their struggles.

Most people see only with their eyes. They are flooded with ego — and ego is nothing more than weakness masquerading as strength. Their preoccupation with their own desires and aspirations blinds them to the needs and fears of others. This hinders their ability to *connect* and garner the support they need, which sabotages their success and exacerbates their fears, anger and anxieties.

YOUR RELATIONSHIPS:
THE KEY TO UNDERSTANDING

Every human being is a big, tender bundle of fears — they fear missing out, looking foolish, getting ripped off, being left behind, being out of control, not being recognized, not being good enough. No one escapes — fear is inherent to us all.

When someone's behavior appears inappropriate, don't be quick to judge, chastise or condemn. Engage your spirit of Magnanimity. Recognize that such behavior usually stems from insecurity and is a cry for attention. Ask yourself, "What fear is he shielding with this behavior?" Then ask, "How can I best alleviate these fears?"

Search for these answers in every encounter — whether you are selling, negotiating, managing, leading, coaching, parenting, campaigning or even romancing.

Look for the fear, the pain, the struggle within — and you will see the key to the individual.

This in turn, will lead you to the hidden rewards of the Wisdom of Magnanimity.

YOUR RELATIONSHIPS:
THE HIDDEN REWARDS

Looking into the heart of others and helping them transcend their fears and anxieties is a very powerful thing to do, not just for others but for yourself as well.

You may not want to admit it, but like everyone else, you harbor a delicate combination of fears and anxieties. Even in your unwillingness to admit it aloud, you are like everyone else.

Your Wisdom of Magnanimity is your key to transcending these worries and insecurities — and the inevitable obstacles and problems that will come your way.

Focus on gaining a deep understanding of others. Look for the role you can play in making their world a better place, and you will find that your passion for this purpose crowds out your own fears and anxieties.

There is nothing more powerful, more effective or more personally rewarding than making a significant impact on others. And as for financial rewards, there is no better way to generate *sustainable* profits than to steward the deepest needs and anxieties of customers.

There is also nothing more inspiring or more infectious than making a difference in the lives of others. Everyone has a deep-seated desire to leave a personal legacy — and when you pave the way for others to make a difference, you will find that most are quick to jump on the bandwagon.

The Wisdom of Magnanimity puts you on the road to making a difference in the lives of others. It leads to making a difference in your own.

YOUR RELATIONSHIPS:
ENGAGE THEIR HEARTS

As you gain a deeper understanding of the essential core of human nature, you will notice a simple pattern. As humans, we have the ability to think, reason and consider, but most decisions are made with our heart, not our head.

The heart is the real power behind everything we do. It is where our deepest needs, fears and anxieties reside — and ultimately, it influences every decision.

In your interaction with others, engage their heart.

Most people emphasize logic or strategy. They command, demand, preach in the mistaken belief that most decisions are made with the head. But there's always a huge hidden cost when you don't engage their hearts. The cost is they are cautious, guarded, half-hearted — and often resentful.

To touch their hearts, look for what brings them peace of mind, security and a sense of fulfillment. Focus on what excites and inspires them.

YOUR RELATIONSHIPS:
THE BEST TECHNIQUE IS NO TECHNIQUE

One of the most significant benefits of the Wisdom of Magnanimity is that it frees up a tremendous amount of energy which you can rechannel into improving the quality of life for yourself and everyone around you.

Most people recognize at some level that they need to become more effective in connecting with others, and devote enormous energy learning how to do it "right." They study techniques, habits and

how-to formulas, diligently applying them to everything — selling, negotiating, listening, communi-
cating, leadership, parenting, team-building, public
speaking, romance.

Techniques and formulas are energy-draining.
They are also artificial crutches that detract from
reality. We become so focused on remembering and
applying what we have learned, our perspective has
little room for anything else. We lose sight of the
need to *connect*. We lose sight of our innate ability
to *connect*. Even when we put on a perfectly-
enacted performance, it falls flat because others see
it clearly as a performance, void of caring,
compassion and humanity.

When it comes to interacting with others — and
everything you do requires interaction — *relinquish
technique*. Release your need to do it right. *There is
no right.* Open your heart and *be yourself.*

You are never more vibrant than when you are
vulnerable, never more genuine than when you are
humble, never more trustworthy than when you are
completely open.

Releasing your reliance on techniques and
formulas opens your perspective to see the other

person completely. They instinctively *feel* your respect and understanding — and when they know how much you care, they care about what you have to say and willingly forgive any imperfections in *how* you say it.

In other words, what you say with your heart communicates far more eloquently than your actual words or style.

Accessing
THE WISDOM OF MAGNANIMITY

(1)   I will reflect on how I look at all the people I encounter today. I will look deep into their hearts to understand their insecurities, fears struggles and aspirations.

(2)   I will ask myself — What role can I play in alleviating the struggle of each person I encounter?

(3)   I will focus on being myself so that I can *connect* with every individual I encounter.

(4)   I will look for ways to engage the heart of others. I will look for what inspires and excites them.

The Wisdom

of

Stratification

*Make
every moment
count*

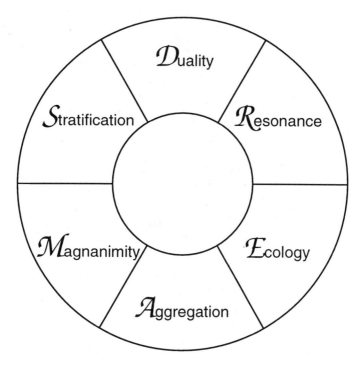

*Every moment
nature starts
on the longest journey,
and every moment
she reaches her goal.*

Johann Wolfgang Von Goethe

The sixth step to waking up your wisdom is looking at each moment as the most important moment of your life.

Stratification comes from the word *Stratify,* which means "to separate or sift into layers." With the Wisdom of Stratification, you sift through everything — and see each moment as though it carries a huge sign proclaiming, "I am the most important moment of your life." This focuses you unwaveringly on the individual, event or task before you in each moment.

Stratification is nature's secret for being both efficient and effective. Observe nature in action, and you will see that nature does nothing inattentively. Every moment, every action, every step is orchestrated to create the *most productive outcome possible.* Every available resource is mobilized, every necessary ally is commissioned to ensure success — and survival.

The roots of a tree are focused unwaveringly on locating every possible drop of water. An owl perched on a limb appears still, but it is constantly alert to the slightest disturbance. Inside the human body, armies of cells roam, vigilant to any unfriendly germ or virus.

Nature exacts a very high price for inattentiveness. If the attention of a tree, bird or cell is scattered for even a moment, it will whither, weaken or vanish. It's all about survival.

If you want to create a meaningful future for yourself, emulate nature. Pay undivided attention to every moment — and *make every moment count.*

The Wisdom of Stratification brightens every moment in three ways:

First, you gain an enlightened view of each moment.

Second, you enjoy and create treasured moments in your relationships.

And the third revelation of the Wisdom of Stratification navigates you through an uncertain future and speeds up your results.

Your Universe:
Triumphant Moments

The first revelation of the Wisdom of Stratification gives you an enlightened view of each and every moment.

In nature, the species that triumph — and survive — leverage every moment. Ants pull thirty times their own weight. Viruses multiply so fast, in a matter of moments they establish an impenetrable beachhead. Deer always move in herds to improve their chances of survival. A eucalyptus grove interweaves its branches into a formidable umbrella, thus blocking the sunlight from any competing plants.

Look behind every triumph of nature and you will see that the secret lies in leveraging and multiplying.

In every moment ask yourself, "How can I make this moment completely worthwhile? How can I leverage my efforts?" Imagine tossing a stone into a pond — the ripples follow each other all the way to the edge. Be alert to every possibility of making such a difference.

Stratify in every moment. Even when repeating a task already made better, ask the questions *again*. Build upon each moment, reinforcing and amplifying everything you do.

Do this and in a sense, you will *create* each moment. And in the process, you will create your own joy, ecstacy and fulfillment.

YOUR UNIVERSE:
MAKE IT WORTHWHILE

Every day and moment, we have many balls in the air. We are hounded by mounting tasks, pressing problems and insistent people, each demanding our attention more urgently than the previous one.

Each moment, we must decide, "Should I continue doing what I am doing?" or "Should I switch gears to the new demand?"

When confronted with such dilemmas — and these dilemmas confront everyone — most people decide to switch gears. They flit from one task to the next, never stopping long enough to make a difference. What they don't realize is that switching gears so often is *the reason* they still tread water.

Each time they switch gears — and most people do it far more often than they realize — they pay a huge price in wasted energy, unnecessary disappointment and mounting frustration.

When the Wisdom of Stratification is in your perspective, more than ninety percent of such dilemmas become *non*-dilemmas.

Stratification means making each moment completely worthwhile. Most distractions diminish the worth of the present moment. Simply ignore them.

Few demands offer opportunities substantially greater than what you are pursuing in the moment. When they present themselves, respond with a quick, unwavering decision.

Give each moment its due — and each moment will build upon the prior moments and multiply into a tremendous advantage for you.

Your Relationships:
Treasured Moments

The second revelation of the Wisdom of Stratification is the secret for creating treasured moments in your relationships.

The quality of a relationship hinges on the attention each person gives to the other. It doesn't matter who starts — if one person treats the other as the most important person of the day, this glow of attention will inevitably ignite a reflecting glow in the other person.

This is a quality inherent in every human — we tend to reflect the feelings that others silently broadcast to us. If we feel respected, we reflect respect back. If we feel disrespected, we reflect that as well.

To create a mutually-respectful relationship with everyone you encounter, give them your undivided attention. Undivided attention means that you totally disallow anything to distract you. Your attention is unshakably devoted to the person you are with. You see their every movement, twitch and blink. You can tell the exact shade and shape of their eyes. They feel the warm glow of your attention. You create a mindful connection.

Most of us don't realize how often we treat others as unimportant. Nor are we aware of the price we pay. Managers "listen" to employees while *they continue working.* Spouses greet each other with little more than a "hello honey." And through the technology of call waiting, we send silent messages to others that they are not as important as the person on the other line.

What starts as a little inattention mushrooms into a cloud of chaos and grief — employees feel unneeded, spouses unappreciated and customers unheard. When they react "inappropriately," we lose sight of what caused this grief in the first place and blame everyone but ourselves.

Without the Wisdom of Stratification, we live in delusion. We believe we are efficient in our relationships — but in reality, we are increasingly *ineffective.* In our struggle to get more done in less time and clean our plate, we inadvertently pile our plate even higher.

YOUR RESULTS:
PLANS AND STRATEGIES

The third revelation of the Wisdom of Stratification navigates you through an uncertain future and speeds up your results.

Conventional wisdom says think before you act. But conventional wisdom typically ignores the reality of the universe.

In nature, thinking and acting are *one and the same*. That's because speed and agility are everything, and the penalty for not acting quickly is final and irreversible.

The roots of a tree can't just think about searching for water — they must do what needs to get done. An owl can't just think about hunting for prey — it must do what needs to get done. The cells in the body can't just think about fending off germs — they must do what needs to get done.

Many people miss this fundamental reality. They pour energy into thinking, talking, planning, analyzing, strategizing, idea-generating, making decisions and getting ready to get ready. Weeks or months slip by, but what needs to be done doesn't get done.

When they finally act, ninety-five percent of their well-laid plans and strategies turn out to be impractical. That's because uncertainty rules the world — no one knows for sure what will work and what won't.

There is only one way to navigate successfully and quickly through the uncertainty inherent in the future. Emulate the Stratification secret of nature. Think and act simultaneously. Think about the best way to act … and at the same time, act to see if your thinking is on track. Pay undivided attention to what happens as you act. Learn what works and what doesn't *in the real world.* Incorporate what you learn immediately into your thinking.

Make every moment truly count — and you will accomplish in weeks what others struggle to accomplish in months.

Accessing
THE WISDOM OF STRATIFICATION

(1) Today, I will look at each individual I encounter as the most important person I will meet during the day.

(2) When I work on a task, I will do it with one-pointed attention. I will look for ways to make each moment completely worthwhile and create the most productive outcome possible. I will ask myself, "Is there a way to do it better?"

(3) I will *simultaneously* look for how to best act, and act so I can best see.

The Wisdom

of

Enlightenment

*See what you can learn
and
learn from what you see*

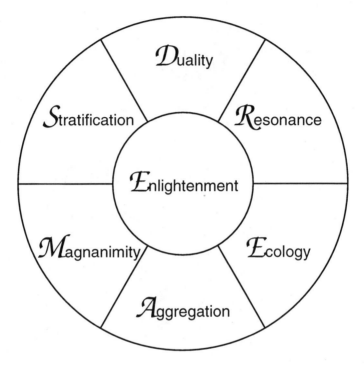

The greatest obstacle
to discovery
is not ignorance.
It is the illusion
of knowledge.

Daniel J Boorstin

The seventh step to waking up your inborn wisdom is learning from everything you see.

The word *Enlightened* means to be informed, illuminated — engaged in *learning*. With the Wisdom of Enlightenment, you look at everything around you and see what you can learn. You learn from nature. You learn from people. You learn from events. You learn about life. And you learn *how to learn.*

Learning is as vital to life as oxygen and water. In nature, the species that thrive are constantly learning, adapting and growing. They go through a never-ending process of reinventing and strengthening themselves.

Anything that stops learning becomes stale, stagnant and weak. When you choose to stop learning, you choose to choke your own life-support system.

Look for the lesson within everything — *learn what life tries to teach you* — and you will free up a huge reservoir of time and energy that is otherwise wasted visiting the same lessons over and over again. Rechannel this energy into learning and growing — and creating the future you want.

Your Universe:
Knowledge and Experience

The first revelation of the Wisdom of Enlightenment sheds a different light on knowledge and experience.

Conventional wisdom says, "Knowledge is power" and "Experience is the best teacher." But the reality is that most people — despite all their degrees, titles and certificates, despite all the books, tapes, seminars and the internet, despite all their years — are neither powerful nor insightful. That's because they typically do not *process* their knowledge or experience.

When you process your knowledge or experience, you transform your life at the most fundamental level. Instead of merely accumulating books, degrees or years on the job, you focus on deepening your understanding of how the world works. Instead of merely knowing more, you know *better*. You gain insight and foresight. In other words, you gain wisdom.

To process knowledge and experience, ask yourself, "How can I use this to enhance my perspective?" Then ask, "Which of my seven wisdoms still needs a nudge?"

YOUR UNIVERSE:
LEARNING AND GROWING

The biggest obstacle between you and Enlightenment is *not* what you have yet to learn. It is what you *think* you have learned, but haven't.

To maximize learning, open your mind. Look at every situation with a spirit of inquiry. Be willing to give up what you have already learned. Discard the should's and shouldn'ts, the do's and don'ts passed down by parents, gurus, teachers and experts. Strip away ego and judgment.

Whenever ego or judgment clouds your perspective, learning stops. You become so focused on proving what you think you know, you are blind to what you *don't* know.

There is a simple way to test if you are truly learning and growing — check your level of discomfort.

Our habits and beliefs have a way of reassuring and comforting us. We aren't even aware that they limit our perspective. But they do. This is why some of the most dazzling breakthroughs are discovered, not by those who are experts in the field, but by people who know so little about the field that their expertise doesn't cloud their perspective.

If you aren't feeling *un*comfortable, it means you're probably not breaking new ground — you're probably not learning and growing.

Your Universe:
Errors and Mistakes

It may sound counter-intuitive, but the fastest way to Enlightenment is to make mistakes — and to make them *fast*. Mistakes are an unavoidable reality of life — no one escapes them. In nature, the sturdiest species make mistakes more often than the rest. They also learn and grow from these mistakes faster than the rest.

Mistakes accelerate the whole process of learning. Don't try to dodge them — it's futile. Don't hide from them. Don't look for someone to blame.

Instead, welcome mistakes, inspect them, review them *quickly* and see what you can learn.

This perspective is particularly important when things go terribly wrong — such as getting fired from a job, dumped by a lover, or rejected by a customer. Your instinctive reaction might be to discount or disregard the oppressing person. But if you do that, you will miss one of the most important opportunities to learn about yourself. *In honor of your own learning*, swallow your pride and see what you can learn. Learn about yourself and learn what you still need to learn.

Your Relationships:
A Growing Bond

The second revelation of the Wisdom of Enlightenment is your key to forging a solid bond with everyone.

There's something valuable for you to learn from every individual who enters your life. When you look for that lesson, you lay the foundation for an exquisite, mutually-fulfilling relationship.

First, being alert to what another person can teach you means you pay silent homage to his entire life — a very respectful thing to do.

You also offer him the opportunity to personally invest himself in you. When an individual invests himself in you by helping and teaching you, he becomes like a gardener tending his garden or a mother nurturing her child. He can't help but feel a growing loyalty and fondness for you.

Over time, the respect becomes mutual and the loyalty deepens. And for little more than a willingness to learn, you forge a lasting bond with everyone in your life — parents, children, friends, family, employers, employees, suppliers and customers.

Your Relationships:
A Lifelong Journey

We are all on a lifelong journey of learning. Many recognize this, but most don't — which explains why so many fail to process the lessons life offers them. Still others mistakenly pursue tricks and techniques, and focus on knowing more, rather than knowing better.

A surprisingly large number of people struggle to change the world around them. What they don't realize is that the disappointments and frustrations in their lives can only be solved where they first originated — in *how they see the world.*

In your journey through life, you will encounter many such individuals.

When you do, do not strut, posture or judge. Instead, recognize that they simply haven't had the opportunity to go through the waking-up process that you have. Recognize that they are now where you were just a short while ago.

Invite them to start a journey of learning and discovery.

If they resist, don't denounce them. Ask yourself if there is something you still need to learn about earning the trust of others. Then, extend your invitation again.

If they agree, do not attempt to change them — there's nothing to change. Simply show them how vital it is to see the world as it really is. Do not share your own insights. Show them how to be insightful on their own.

Point to the clues of nature — the exquisite coexistence of opposites (Duality), the inherent rhythm of life (Resonance), the never-ending cycles (Ecology), the underlying interdependencies (Aggregation), the inevitable struggles that engulf everyone (Magnanimity), the imperative to make every moment count (Stratification) and the necessity to continuously learn and grow (Enlightenment).

Something powerful happens whenever you share these clues of nature.

Each time you enlighten another, you inevitably learn something new yourself — it's part of the process. You see the world with greater clarity, identify blind spots you didn't know you had and uncover even deeper insights. And you experience the true ecstacy that comes from knowing you made a difference in a fellow human's life.

Accessing
THE WISDOM OF ENLIGHTENMENT

(1)   Today, I will reflect on how I process knowledge, education and experience. In everything that happens, do I see what I can learn? Do I learn from what I see?

(2)   I will honor learning — I will take every lesson life offers me and learn from it. I will use mistakes as a tool to learn and grow. And when I feel uncomfortable with a situation, I will reflect on what I have yet to learn.

(3)   With every individual who enters my life, I will look for the opportunity to learn something new.

(4)   When I encounter someone who doesn't know what I know, I will invite them to begin a journey of learning and discovery.

A New Beginning

Wisdom is destiny.

How you see the world governs your thoughts ... which governs your character ... which governs your destiny.

You now stand at the threshold of your wisdom — the threshold of your destiny. If you want a life of abiding joy and abundance, wake up your wisdom and see things as they are. Become aligned with the truth of life and the universe.

There is a simple, non-intrusive process for spontaneously, even automatically, seeing things as they are. Identify a five-minute period each day when you are mentally alone and able to reflect — such as commuting, jogging, showering or brushing.

During those five minutes, reflect back on any pivotal moment of the previous twenty-four hours.

Reflect on your perspective during that moment and how it affected your thoughts, actions and results. Now, examine that same moment through the prism of Duality and reflect on how this perspective might have led you to act more wisely — and how the outcome might have been more gratifying and long-lasting as a result.

While reflecting, don't regret what happened. Do not judge yourself. Simply observe, and this observation in itself will clarify your perspective for the next time.

The next day, repeat the process, this time through the prism of Resonance. Continue each day until you have reflected upon all seven wisdoms. Then, start again.

A remarkable thing happens when you observe this way each day. You see the world with a new clarity and insight. You see hidden qualities in others you blindly took for granted. You see hidden opportunities you never knew existed. You see hidden obstacles before they become insurmountable. You see and enjoy a world most never see.

Remember, when you change how you see the world, your whole world changes.

Acknowledgements

This book would not have been possible without all the people I have encountered in my life. I learned something significant about myself and the world from each and everyone of you. I feel privileged that you entered my life. Thank you.

It is impossible to acknowledge a lifetime of individuals in this space. But I must specifically acknowledge those who first taught me the immense power in seeing the world as it is — My loving mother Shrimati Gopi Motwane, dearest father Shri Arjan Motwane and best friend and sister Shalini Wadhwani. Thank you for lovingly nurturing and nourishing me and showing me a world I didn't know existed.

I also feel a deep gratitude to those individuals who stewarded the production of this book:

Mike Aguilera, Scott Arthur, Rita Connor, Richard Deutsch, Barbara Firth, Paul Gross, Jaffer Habib, Patty Hastings, William Huffman, Gloria McGahey, Maria Ruiz, Curt and Kay Strate, Stan Unger, Elaine Whittington, Sally Wright — thank you very much for taking time from your busy schedules to give your valuable feedback.

Sandy Webb — thank you for your editorial expertise.

Janine Lechuga — thank you for your unabashed enthusiasm for this project. It truly is a "labor of love."

Daniel Erickson — thank you for all the caring evenings and weekends you devoted to help bring out the message with maximum clarity. Without you, this book wouldn't be as accessible as it is. Thank you also for your undying faith in me and encouraging me to start this project.

Personal Note

Just as nature is perfect in its imperfections, so are we. Perfection, as we think of it in the traditional sense, is an illusion, not reality.

I am glaringly aware of my own imperfections, human frailties and vulnerabilities. I often struggle and stumble. I am humbled by how much I yet have to learn.

But this does not slow me down. It empowers me. There is nothing more exhilarating than knowing I have a life full of learning and growing ahead of me. Also, there is nothing more gratifying to me than looking at the world through my heart and soul. My hope with this book is to make a world of difference, one person at a time — and also, a difference in the world.

Wisdom Resources

A variety of different resources are available for waking up the Power of your Wisdom. For FREE information, check your selections below and return this page or a copy of this page.

- ❏ *Power of Wisdom* Newsletter
- ❏ *Power of Wisdom* Workshops
- ❏ *Power of Wisdom* Support Groups in your community
- ❏ *Power of Wisdom* Seminars specifically tailored for your company or association
- ❏ Quantity discounts for bulk purchases for sales promotions, premiums or fund-raising
- ❏ Wisdom Quotient — 360° feedback from your family, friends and co-workers
- ❏ *Power of Wisdom* T-Shirts
- ❏ *Power of Wisdom* Posters
- ❏ *Power of Wisdom* Postcards

Name _____

Company _____

Address _____

City _____ State ____ Zip _____

Phone _____ Fax _____ e-mail _____

Visit our web site at http//www.powerofwisdom.com

The Wisdom Institute, P.O. Box 8004, Redondo Beach, CA 90277
Phone: 1-877-76WISDOM, Fax: 1-310-944-9880

Free Wisdom Card

As a gift to readers of *The Power of Wisdom*, we are making available a FREE wallet-sized reminder card listing the seven principles of wisdom. These cards are tailored to your specific personal and professional objectives.

For your FREE card, please check your objective below and return this page or a copy of this page. Only ONE card per household or address, please.

- ❏ *Power of Wisdom* Card (overall)
- ❏ *Power of Wisdom* Card for Relationships
- ❏ *Power of Wisdom* Card for Creativity
- ❏ *Power of Wisdom* Card for Leadership
- ❏ *Power of Wisdom* Card for Teamwork
- ❏ *Power of Wisdom* Card for Small Business

- ❏ Check here for information about ordering more cards

Name _____

Company _____

Address _____

City _____ State _____ Zip _____

Phone _____ Fax _____ e-mail _____

Visit our web site at http//www.powerofwisdom.com

The Wisdom Institute, P.O. Box 8004, Redondo Beach, CA 90277
Fax: 1-310-944-9880 (Fax or mail requests only, no phone calls please)